# Thomas Jefferson

## Father of the Declaration of Independence

Thomas loved the outdoors, especially hiking and riding.

Thomas was born on his family's farm in Shadwell, Virginia on April 13, 1743. Thomas' father was a farmer and surveyor. His mother was from one of the finest families in the state. Thomas was tall and thin with reddish-blond hair and a freckled face that sunburnt easily.

To learn more about Thomas, unscramble the words in the sentences below!

Thomas was the _____ of ten

HDITR

(rhymes with heard)

children. He had a _____

NWNIGNI

(rhymes with spinning)

personality and a big _____.

LMSIE

(rhymes with pie)

Thomas was expected to grow up to be a Virginia gentleman. To do this, he had to study, learn to play the violin, and dance the minuet and the Virginia reel.

The minuet was a slow, graceful dance. The Virginia reel was a lively, folk dance.

Color the picture of the dancers.

Thomas' favorite school subject was language! By age 9, Thomas had studied Greek, Latin, and French.

Growing up, Thomas was very well-educated. He chose the College of William and Mary in Williamsburg to continue his studies. He became interested in the law and served as an apprentice to an attorney. He also became a member of the Virginia legislature.

Thomas grew up to be a tall, muscular man with a high-speaking voice.

**How old was Thomas when his father died? Solve the math problem to find out.**

1757 (year his father died)

- 1743 (year Thomas was born)

(age at his father's death)

In 1757, Thomas' father died, leaving many slaves and thousands of acres of land. Until Thomas was old enough to manage the plantation, an adult guardian took over.

Thomas was interested in a variety of things, from music to law to dance. But one of his most favorite things was architecture. He said, "putting up and pulling down" were one of his favorite pastimes. He started building a home on a small mountain on his property.

Color Thomas' home.

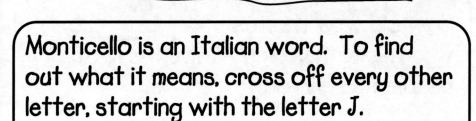

Monticello is an Italian word. To find out what it means, cross off every other letter, starting with the letter J.

J L U I R T M T E L W E N M
I O X U S N L T S A P I V N

Monticello means __ __ __ __ __ __

__ __ __ __ __ __ __ __ __.

Thomas named his home Monticello.

In 1770, Thomas met Martha Wayles Skelton. She was a 22-year-old pretty widow with a baby son and a large estate. Martha had several admirers, but Thomas stole her heart with his intelligence, personality, and love of music. They were married in 1772.

**Color the wedding bells.**

**With relations between England and America strained, a war began brewing. Which war was this? Circle the correct answer.**

Civil War

Revolutionary War

Vietnam War

During this time, England had increased taxes on the colonies, but would not allow the colonists to govern themselves. This caused many bad feelings between Britain and the American colonies.

During the beginning of the Revolutionary War, the 32-year-old Thomas traveled to Philadelphia to help write the Declaration of Independence. The American colonies were making a statement that they no longer wanted to be a part of Great Britain. Signing this document was considered treason by the British, and any signers caught were to be put to death!

While Thomas was governor, he worked hard to pass a law guaranteeing freedom of religion. Although a slave owner, Thomas also tried to abolish slavery. His attempt was not successful.

During the Revolutionary War, Thomas served as governor of Virginia.

**THOMAS    MARTHA    WAR**

| | | | |
|---|---|---|---|
| V | J | S | E |
| O | I | H | A |
| S | C | R | S |
| A | T | U | G |
| M | F | W | R |
| O | B | L | S |
| H | W | G | J |
| T | U | M | A |

After the war, Thomas served as America's minister to France. He lived in Paris for awhile until he was called back to the states to serve as President George Washington's Secretary of State. In 1793, he left this position to go back home to Monticello to remodel his house and work on his farm.

## VIRGINIA    WRITER

| | | | |
|---|---|---|---|
| W | P | Z | Q |
| B | L | M | G |
| N | R | F | T |
| D | V | O | C |
| I | T | E | R |
| O | N | K | U |
| L | D | I | S |
| R | T | H | A |

**Find the words in the Word Find.**

At the end of the war, Martha Jefferson died a few months after giving birth. The heart-broken Thomas never remarried.

In 1796, Thomas was called back to Washington to serve as Vice-president under John Adams. Then, in 1800, he defeated Adams and became the third president of the United States. He called his position as president a "splendid misery."

## Match the words below to find three of Jefferson's nicknames.

Father of                  Monticello

Sage of                    the Declaration of Independence

Man of                     the People

Thomas was very popular as president. He served two terms, from 1801 to 1809.

Thomas was often bothered with migraine headaches.

**Color the United States flag.**

During his presidency, Thomas bought a large amount of land from France. This new land, known as the Louisiana Purchase, doubled the size of the country! After his second term as president, Thomas happily retired to Monticello.

*During retirement, Thomas founded a public university in Virginia.*

Louisiana Purchase

**What was the name of the university Jefferson founded? Solve the code to find out!**

| A | B | C | D | E | F | G | H | I | J | K | L | M |
|---|---|---|---|---|---|---|---|---|---|---|---|---|
| ☀ | ❀ | ✣ | ♣ | ➢ | ♥ | ❗ | ✳ | ✂ | ✆ | ☛ | ✈ | ✉ |

| N | O | P | Q | R | S | T | U | V | W | X | Y | Z |
|---|---|---|---|---|---|---|---|---|---|---|---|---|
| ✿ | ☆ | ◆ | ✡ | ✎ | ❥ | ☎ | ⊷ | ✚ | ✖ | ✍ | ✠ | ✓ |

Thomas Jefferson died on July 4, 1826, exactly 50 years after the Declaration of Independence was signed. He will be forever remembered as a talented and beloved founding father of America.

John Adams, second president of the U.S. and the only other president to sign the Declaration of Independence, also died the same day as Jefferson!

**Write F if the statement is a FACT and O if it is an OPINION.**

\_\_\_\_\_ Jefferson was the greatest president.

\_\_\_\_\_ Jefferson wrote the Declaration of Independence.

\_\_\_\_\_ Jefferson married Martha Skelton.

\_\_\_\_\_ Jefferson enjoyed being president.

Jefferson's picture is featured on the nickel and the two-dollar bill.

# Glossary

**apprentice:** a person who is learning a trade by helping a person skilled in that trade

**architecture:** the science or work of planning and putting up buildings

**draft:** a plan, sketch, or drawing of something to be built or done

**misery:** a condition in which a person suffers greatly or is very unhappy

**surveyor:** a person whose job is to measure the size, shape, and boundaries of a piece of land

**treason:** the act or an instance of betraying one's country

# Pop Quiz!

1. Thomas' home in Virginia was called:
   - ○ Monticello
   - ○ Mount Vernon
   - ○ Warm Springs

2. Thomas went to college at:
   - ○ University of Virginia
   - ○ Harvard
   - ○ College of William and Mary

3. Thomas is famous for writing the:
   - ○ Gettysburg Address
   - ○ Declaration of Independence
   - ○ Bible

4. Thomas founded this college:
   - ○ University of Virginia
   - ○ Washington University
   - ○ Jefferson College

5. As governor of Virginia, Thomas created a law guaranteeing freedom of:
   - ○ speech
   - ○ religion
   - ○ taxes